Hair There and Everywhere

By Karin Luisa Badt

CHILDRENS PRESS®
CHICAGO

Picture Acknowledgements
Cover (top left), NASA; Cover (top right), © Lawrence Migdale/Tony Stone Images; Cover (bottom left), Photri; Cover (bottom right), © Kennon Cooke/Valan; 1 H. Armstrong Roberts; 3 (top), © Cameramann International Ltd.; 3 (center), © H. Heinzen/SuperStock International, Inc.; 3 (bottom), © Wu Gang/Photri; 4 (top), © T. Ulrich/H. Armstrong Roberts; 4 (bottom), North Wind Picture Archives; 5, The Bettmann Archive; 6 (left), © Wendy Stone/Odyssey/Frerck/Chicago; 6 (right), © Motor-Presse International/SuperStock International, Inc.; 7 (top), H. Armstrong Roberts; 7 (bottom left), © Abbey Sea/Unicorn Stock Photos; 7 (bottom right), © Jeff Greenberg/Unicorn Stock Photos; 8 (2 photos), H. Armstrong Roberts; 9 (top), © Cameramann International, Ltd.; 9 (bottom), © Wu Gang/Photri; 9 (right), H. Armstrong Roberts; 10 (top), © Fred Bruemmer/Valan; 10 (bottom), © Anna E. Zuckerman/PhotoEdit; 11 (left), UPI/Bettmann; 11 (top right), © Marcus Brooke/Tony Stone Images; 11 (bottom right), © John Cancalosi/Valan; 12 (top), © Chris Harvey/Tony Stone Images; 12 (bottom), Tony Stone Images; 13 (top), H. Armstrong Roberts; 13 (bottom), © Barry Barker/Odyssey/Frerck/Chicago; 14 (left), Edward Curtis Collection/Odyssey/Frerck/Chicago; 14 (right), © Noriyuki Yoshida/SuperStock International, Inc.; 15 (left), © Bill Aron/PhotoEdit; 15 (right), UPI/Bettmann; 16 (top), © A.K.G., Berlin/SuperStock International, Inc.; 16 (bottom), © Jason Laure; 17 (left), Stock Montage; 17 (top right), © H. Armstrong Roberts; 17 (bottom right), The Bettmann Archive; 18 (top), © Jeff Greenberg/Unicorn Stock Photos; 18 (bottom), AP/Wide World Photos; 19 (left), © Tom Rosenthal/SuperStock International, Inc.; 19 (right), UPI/Bettmann; 20 (left), United Nations; 20 (top right), © Cameramann International, Ltd.; 20 (center right), © David Austen/Tony Stone Images; 20 (bottom right), © Mark Richards/PhotoEdit; 21 (left), © Hilarie Kavanagh/Tony Stone Images; 21 (right), © Robert Frerck/Odyssey/Frerck/Chicago; 22 (top), Stock Montage; 22 (bottom), H. Armstrong Roberts; 23, UPI/Bettmann; 24-25 (top), © Alan Greeley/Photri; 24 (center), © Jason Laurè; 24 (bottom), AP/Wide World Photos; 25 (top right), © Carl Purcell; 25 (bottom), H. Armstrong Roberts; 26 (top), © Rick Rusing/Tony Stone Images; 26 (bottom), © David Young-Wolff/Tony Stone Images; 27 (left), © John Cancalosi/Valan; 27 (right), © William Thompson/Bettmann; 28 (top), UPI/Bettmann; 28 (bottom), © Carl Purcell; 29 (top left), © Jane P. Downton/Root Resources; 29 (top right), © Irene Hubbell/Root Resources; 29 (bottom left), AP/Wide World Photos; 29 (bottom right), © Kennon Cooke/Valan; 30 (top), © Robert Frerck/Odyssey/Frerck/Chicago; 30 (bottom), © Ron Dahlquist/Superstock International Inc.; 31 (top left), © Rich Baker/Unicorn Stock Photos; 31 (top center), © Jason Laurè; 31 (top right), © Cameramann International, Ltd.; 31 (bottom left), © Buddy Mays/Travel Stock; 31 (bottom right), © Jeff Greenberg/Unicorn Stock Photos

On the cover
Top: American kids with a variety
  of hairstyles
Bottom left: Fulani man, Nigeria
Bottom right: Plains Indian woman,
  United States

On the title page
An 1800s photograph of American women
with unusually long hair

Project Editor Shari Joffe
Design Beth Herman Design Associates
Photo Research Feldman & Associates

Badt, Karin Luisa.
    Hair There and Everywhere / by Karin Luisa Badt.
        p. cm. — (A World of Difference)
    Includes index.
    ISBN 0-516-08187-X
    1. Hair — Juvenile literature. 2. Hairstyles — Juvenile literature.
  I. Title. II. Series.
  GT2290.B33 1994
  391`.5 — dc20
                           94-11652
                             CIP
                             AC

Contents

The Magic of Hair

What do these things have in common?

- Whiskers on kittens
  - Quills on a porcupine
    - That stuff on top of your head

The answer is: they're all HAIR! All mammals—including cats, porcupines, and humans—have hair. Like a blanket or a sun umbrella, hair protects your skin from the cold and heat. It also protects your skin against moisture. When it rains, your hair may get a little damp, but your scalp probably doesn't get soaked—unless, of course, you like to play outside in the rain! Hair protects in other ways, too. A cat's whiskers are very sensitive to touch. They help the cat feel its way through narrow or dark places. And you know what happens to any animal that tries to bite a porcupine: a snoutful of sharp quills! Hair is an amazing thing. It is part of you, but unlike an arm or a leg, you can snip it off and it will grow back again! In fact, your hair will grow all your life, even after you have stopped growing. Just like magic!

Samson The Bible tells of a man named Samson, who had tremendous strength because of his long hair.

4

Hair's ability to keep growing may be the reason why, in many cultures of the world, hair is believed to have special powers. In Nigeria, children born with thick, curly hair are thought to bring good luck to their parents. In some parts of India, people cut a lock of their hair and offer it to God in the hope that God will then grant them favors. People who live in the region of Mount Hagen in Papua New Guinea believe that the spirits of your ancestors live in your hair. If your hair grows well, it means that the ancestors like you.

In many cultures, the hair you cut off is considered a special part of you, even though it's no longer attached to you. In Europe and the United States, people sometimes keep a loved one's lock of hair in a locket. In the Middle East, Muslims used to save all the hair they lost throughout their life, and have it buried with them when they died.

The Bible tells of a man named Samson, who is stronger than all the other men in the world—because of his long hair! When Samson's enemies learn his secret, they cut off his hair in the middle of the night. Poor Samson loses all his strength. But his hair grows back, and . . . guess what? He is strong once again.

Rapunzel, Rapunzel, let down your hair! The fairy-tale heroine Rapunzel really *depended* on her long hair. The handsome prince used it as a ladder so he could climb up into her room and save her!

Let Your Hair Down!

Perhaps the most magical thing about hair is that it expresses something about who you are. What's *your* hair like? Maybe you have straight red hair, frizzy black hair, or short purple hair! Have you ever considered what your hair says about you?

United States

A world of difference The wonderful thing about human hair is that it comes in many different colors, thicknesses, textures, and lengths. It may be red, black, blonde, brown, white, or grey; fine or thick; and curly, kinky, wavy, or straight. Also, a person can shave it off, or grow it very, very long!

Masai girl, Kenya

It never stops growing . . .

Hair is one part of your body that always keeps growing. A few people, such as the women in this 1800s photograph, have grown their hair to *really* unusual lengths.

Sulawesi, Indonesia

Norway

Combing through Cultures

Sometimes, you can actually tell where someone is from by the way they wear their hair. The world is home to thousands of different cultural groups, many of which have their own special hairstyles. A special hairstyle does two things: it helps identify a group as being separate from other groups, and it helps give members of the same group a sense of belonging.

In the Andes Mountains of Ecuador, Peru, and Bolivia, Indian women tend to wear two thick braids and a bowler hat on top. In New Zealand, the traditional hairstyle for Maori men is a topknot with a single white feather sticking up from it. In southwestern Africa, every culture group has its own traditional hairstyle. For example, in Angola, women of the Mwila people wear their hair in hundreds of thin braids around the head, while Mbalantu women wear their hair in thick braids down to the ground. What about you? Do you think people could guess where you're from or what group you belong to by the way you wear your hair?

Yoruba woman, Lagos, Nigeria
In parts of Africa, each culture group has its own traditional hairstyle.

Girls in Sunday dress, Germany This is a hairstyle worn traditionally by girls of the Black Forest region of Germany.

Aymara Indian women, Bolivia The Aymara people live in the Andes Mountains of Bolivia. Traditionally, Aymara women have worn braids and bowler hats.

Kootenai man, North America, late 1800s This was a traditional hairstyle of the Kootenai people, who lived in what is now northwestern Montana, northern Idaho, and south-eastern British Columbia.

Hmong woman, Guizhou Province, China The Hmong, or Miao, are mountain dwellers who live in isolated villages in southern China, Vietnam, Laos, and Thailand. On certain festive days, young women of the Hmong of southwest China's Wumeng Mountains wear an elaborate traditional hairstyle that honors the buffalo, a sacred animal for the Hmong. The girls' real hair—which is sometimes as much as five feet long—is mixed with wool and linen. Then it is wound around a huge comb that is shaped like two buffalo horns. The women take great pride in their hair, and these headdresses become prized family possessions.

Girl's Hair, Boy's Hair

Are you a boy or a girl? Your hairstyle may be a big clue! In most parts of the world, boys and girls wear their hair differently.

Boys always have short hair, and girls always have long hair, right? WRONG! During most periods of history, it was the fashion for boys—and men—to have long hair. In ancient Mesopotamia, both men and women wore their hair all the way down their backs. In nineteenth-century England, little boys wore their hair down to their shoulders. And in France, long ago, the king was required to have long hair. To cut off a king's hair meant to take away his power. Just like Samson!

Kathmandu, Nepal
Some Nepalese men wear their hair long.

Masai girls and boys
The Masai are a nomadic people who live in Kenya and Tanzania. As children, Masai girls wear their heads shaven; Masai boys wear short hair.

Sinhalese man, 1800s Traditionally, many Sinhalese men of Ceylon (now Sri Lanka) wore their hair long.

Boys and girls, China In many cultures throughout the world, it is common to see boys with short hair and girls with longer hair. Of course, this is not always the case. Perhaps you are a boy with long hair or a girl with short hair!

Mayan boy, Chiapas, Mexico Mayan boys wear their hair long.

Young Hair, Old Hair

How often do you see a grandmother in pigtails and bangs? Or what about a little girl with her hair in a bun? Not very often!

People's hairstyles often tell something about their age. This is because in most cultures, people change their hairstyles at various stages of their lives. When people switch to an "older" hairstyle, it identifies them as being part of a new age group. For instance, a Himba boy in Namibia wears his hair in two braids along the sides of his face. As soon as he has enough experience and has proved his independence, he begins wearing one braid on each side of his head. In ancient Egypt, boys wore a lock of hair over one ear to symbolize their youth. This was called the "Horus lock."

Young Samburu warrior, Kenya Among the Samburu people, males are grouped by age sets. From the time they are very small, boys work toward becoming warriors. About every seven years, Samburu males who have proved themselves worthy "graduate" from one age set to the next. Each time a male moves to the next age grouping, he changes his hairstyle. This young man's braided, mud-plastered hair indicates that he is a young warrior.

It was named after the son of the Egyptian goddess Isis. In Italy today, many little girls wear their hair in a ponytail on top of their head. It shoots up like water from a fountain!

In many cultures, when children reach a special age, their hair is cut in a special ceremony. Usually, this symbolizes that the child is entering a new stage of life. He or she now has a new identity as an older person. When a Tchrikin boy in southwestern Africa is eight years old, his family celebrates by cutting his hair for the very first time. There is a similar celebration for Orthodox Jewish boys. They have their first haircut when they are three years old. Among some Orthodox Jewish people, this is done at the festival of Lag B'omer, thirty-three days after Passover.

A bald man It's natural for men to lose hair as they get older. Nevertheless, since ancient times, men have fought to keep their hair. Treatments to prevent baldness have included lotions made of crocodile or snake fat, vinegar, and even dog paws. Most of these lotions do not work! Nature has its way. Some men fight baldness by having hair-transplant surgery. Others settle for a toupee, or hairpiece. And others realize that bald can be beautiful!

Elderly woman, Mexico It is very common for people's hair to turn grey or white as they get older. This happens because their bodies stop producing the pigment that gives hair its color.

Single Hair, Married Hair

A hairstyle may indicate not only your age, but also your marital status: whether you are married or single. This is because in some parts of the world, people wear their hair differently before and after marriage. In many cultures, married women wear their hair in a special way to make it clear that they are no longer available to other men.

Traditional Japanese wedding ceremony Traditionally, young, unmarried girls in Japan wore the *take-simada* hairstyle, while married women wore the *maru-mage* hairstyle.

Hopi girl with squash blossom whorls, 1800s
Traditionally, Hopi girls wore their hair in two big curls—called squash blossom whorls—to show that they were available for marriage.

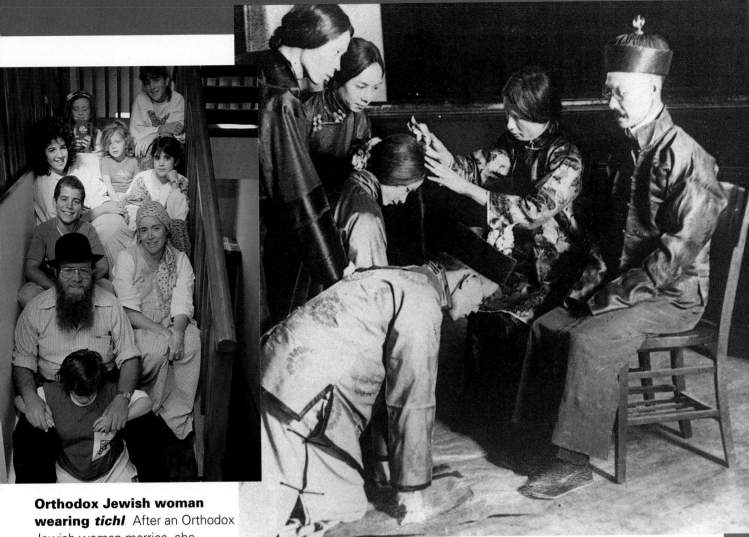

Orthodox Jewish woman wearing *tichl* After an Orthodox Jewish woman marries, she may keep her hair covered with a *sheitel* (wig) or *tichl* (kerchief). This symbolizes her fidelity to her husband.

Chinese wedding ceremony, 1920s In China, young girls who were unmarried traditionally wore their hair in a long braid that hung down their back. When they married, they began wearing their hair pulled back into a low bun.

Until the twentieth century, it was common for unmarried girls in the United States and in many European countries to wear their hair loose. After marriage, they wore it pinned up or covered. Unmarried girls in China wore their hair in one long braid down their back. After they got married, they wore it pulled into a low bun. In many African countries today, a woman's hairstyle shows not only whether she is married or single, but even whether or not she has children.

15

Your Part in Society

Your hair can also say something about your social status: how rich or important you are in your community. Ever since the beginning of human civilization, people have used hair and clothes to express their social position.

In ancient times, noblemen in Sumeria (where Iraq is today) wore gold dust in their hair. Only a rich person could afford to sprinkle gold on themselves! In ancient Egypt, anyone who could afford it shaved their head and wore a wig. Wigs were expensive. People who could not afford wigs covered their heads with caps of felt or leather.

People can also demonstrate their power by the way they wear their hair. Powerful Aztec warriors in Central America during the fourteenth and fifteenth centuries wore only a ridge of hair on their heads, to show they had taken many prisoners. In Japan a few hundred years ago, the wives of the highest-ranking nobles wore the *sage-sitazi* hairstyle, while their ladies-in-waiting wore the *kata-hazusi* hairstyle. It was clear to everyone who had more power! Even today, in Nigeria, the wives of kings of the Yoruba people wear the *suku* hairstyle, which looks like a basket.

Marie Antoinette, late 1700s
As a symbol of her wealth and power, French queen Marie Antoinette wore hairstyles so elaborate that some of them made her more than a foot taller.

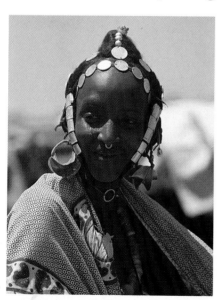

Fulani woman, Mali This market seller is wearing all her silver and gold finery. This lets others know that she is self-sufficient and prosperous.

Ancient Egyptian wall painting 1352 B.C. In ancient Egypt, wealthy men and women shaved their heads and wore highly stylized wigs. This helped protect them from the sun. The men also shaved their faces and, on ceremonial occasions, wore stiff, false beards.

Julius Caesar Among the Gauls, who lived in what is now France, it was a sign of honor to have very long hair. When Roman general Julius Caesar conquered the Gauls in the 50s B.C., he made them cut their hair to show that he was master.

Caricature of 18th-century French hairstyles The French upper classes got so carried away with their elaborate hairstyles that cartoonists of the day began making fun of them!

Hair that Works for You

Sometimes, your hairstyle is influenced by the kind of work you do. Members of a particular profession may style their hair the same way to help other people identify them as belonging to that profession. Ancient Egyptian jugglers and dancers, for example, could be identified by their hair, which they wore short with long braids weighted down with pebbles. In Nigeria today, Yoruba court messengers in the Igbomina kingdom can be recognized by their shaved heads with an oval patch of hair left at the back. And what about modern rock stars? Sometimes their hair is so fantastic that you just *know* they're in the entertainment business!

Sardine factory worker, Estonia For sanitary reasons, people who work in food processing are usually required to cover their hair.

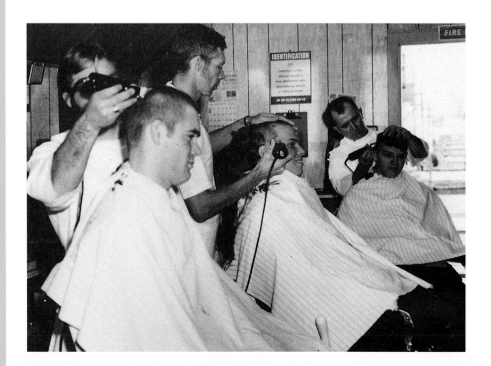

American military haircuts Men in the United States military are required to keep their hair short.

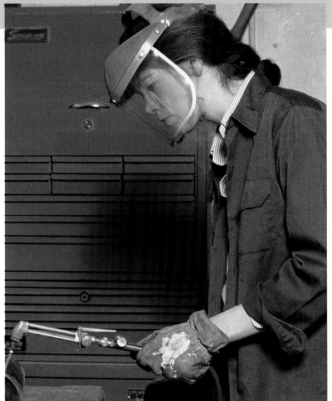

Welder, United States Some workers are required to wear their hair pulled back for safety reasons.

British judge In England, wig shapes once set professional groups apart. Doctors, judges, lawyers, and military officers all wore different kinds of wigs. Even today, British lawyers and judges wear special wigs.

With some jobs, a person is actually required to wear his or her hair a certain way—as part of a uniform. In most cultures, soldiers are required to have the same haircut as the other soldiers in their group. By agreeing to cut their hair the same way, soldiers show that they are obedient to a greater authority: the country they serve. Also, having the same haircut helps soldiers feel that they are part of a unified group—a team working together.

Religious Beliefs

The way you wear your hair may say something about your religious beliefs. Many religions have rules about hairstyles. Some religions require their followers to shave or cover their hair, while others dictate a special hairstyle. Why? Because religions usually stress modesty and humility—and hair is often viewed as a symbol of human vanity. Hair can be so beautiful that it can make people proud of themselves. Also, by following a religion's rules about how to wear one's hair, a person shows that he or she respects and obeys a power higher than himself or herself.

Amish man Amish men, following the doctrine of 17th-century religious leader Jakob Ammann, do not wear moustaches or trim their beards.

Hasidic Jewish man Hasidic Jewish men do not shave, and they wear *pe'ot,* curls of hair that hang in front of the ears. They follow this practice because a section of the Bible states that one should not cut the corners of one's beard.

Palestinian Muslims Some religious Muslim women cover their hair with a veil called a *ghata.* This is because the *Qur'an,* the Muslim holy text, states that women should cover their hair.

Catholic nun Traditionally, all Roman Catholic nuns wore habits with head veils that completely covered their hair. Today, many orders no longer require their members to wear the traditional veil.

Buddhist monks, Thailand A razor is one of the few objects Buddhist monks actually own. Keeping their heads shaven is one of the ways they avoid distraction from their devotion to a spiritual life.

Sikh man, India Sikhs never cut their hair, and they keep it covered with a turban. This shows that they are above such worldly concerns. They also never cut their facial hair. This man is wearing his moustache pinned up. Unrolled, it is more than four feet long!

21

Political Hair

Guiseppe Garibaldi
Italian patriot Guiseppe Garibaldi (1807-82) spent his life trying to unify Italy into one country. Men who supported him wore a beard like his.

As you can see, hairstyles often tell a lot about where people fit into society: their cultural group, their gender, their age and marital status, their occupation, their social status, and their religion. Throughout history, people have also used hair to make political statements.

Sometimes, people wear their hair a certain way to show their support for their government or their society's values. For example, in 1778, French women celebrated a naval victory over the English by wearing small ships in their hair! In 1970, Nigerian women wore a hairstyle known as *ogun pari* to commemorate the end of a Nigerian civil war.

Chinese barber shop, late 1800s For a long time, the traditional hairstyle for Chinese men was a long braid, called a *queue*, that hung down the back. In 1912, the Manchus—the royal family that had ruled China since the middle of the 1600s—were overthrown. The new leaders outlawed the *queue* because it was a symbol of the old ways.

Some governments have *pressured* their citizens into showing their allegiance by telling them how they can or can't wear their hair.

But what about UNCONVENTIONAL hairstyles? Sometimes, to rebel against society, people refuse to wear their hair in a conventional or traditional way. It was once the custom for Malagasy (the name for the people of Madagascar) to cut their hair when a king died, to show that they were sad. In the 1800s, a group of Malagasy wanted to show that they did not want to have a king anymore. So when the king died, they refused to cut their hair. This rebellious group became known as the *Tsimihety:* "Those Who Don't Cut Their Hair."

Woman with 1920s bob
Some people were horrified when, in the 1920s, young American and European women began cutting their hair "boyishly" short. The hairstyle, called the "bob," was a sign that women were beginning to reject their traditional role in society. More and more, they were becoming active in politics and gaining economic power from jobs outside the home.

In the 1960s, many young people in Europe and the United States wore their hair long and wild to protest against the conservative values and politics of their societies. In 1967, the Greek government was so afraid of the influence of these "hippies" that it banned long-haired tourists from entering Greece!

During the same time, a hairstyle called the Afro became popular among African-American men and

1960s hippies

Anti-hippie billboard
This 1960s billboard shows how some members of America's older generation reacted negatively—and quite loudly—to the trend of young men growing their hair long.

Rastafarians The Rastafarians are a group in Jamaica with radical political and religious ideas. They formed in the 1930s to rebel against many of the values of the modern world. Their long, ropelike braids, called dreadlocks, help identify them as a distinct group with a different set of values than others in their society.

British punks The punk movement originated in the 1970s as a form of rebellion by working-class youths in Great Britain. By wearing punk haircuts and clothes, young people expressed their frustration with their position in society.

women. For many people, wearing an Afro expressed pride in one's African roots. Allowing one's hair to be natural instead of straightening it or flattening it was a statement about no longer conforming to "white" standards of beauty. For some people, wearing an Afro also expressed dissatisfaction with the treatment of blacks in the United States.

If you haven't yet made a statement with your hair, maybe you will someday!

Hair for Special Occasions

People often wear special hairstyles on special occasions. This is one way to show how important the occasion is for them. They might never wear their hair the same way again.

Many people wear their hair in an extraordinary way on the day of their wedding. This is because in many cultures, a wedding is one of the most important symbolic events in a person's life. In Namibia, !Xu brides wear ostrich shells, copper beads, and fruit seeds in their hair. In China, brides traditionally had the hair at their hairline removed the day before their wedding. This ceremony, called "the opening of the face" (hoi minh), was to prepare the bride for her new identity as a wife. People also may wear their hair in a special way on sad occasions—such as the death of a loved one—to demonstrate their grief. Changing one's hair symbolizes that the mourner is now a changed person because of his or her loss.

American wedding People may wear a special hairstyle to mark the importance of an event in their lives. In the United States, as in many countries, a woman usually wears her hair a special way on the day of her wedding.

Mexican festival Wearing traditional hairstyles and clothing on special occasions is one way that people celebrate their ethnic heritage.

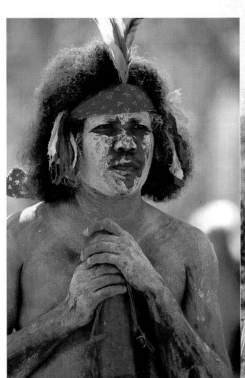

**Aboriginal ceremony,
Australia**

An Angolan woman
whose father has died
wears strings of beads
wrapped around her
hair like a turban. Men of the Mount Hagen region
of Papua New Guinea wear their hair messy and
unwashed if they have the misfortune to lose a son.
Chinese women who are mourning a loved one
often wear white flowers in their hair.

**Ceremonial dancer,
Papua New Guinea** This special
ceremonial wig, made of feathers,
is called the "Bird of Paradise."

Your Crowning Glory

Would you ever have guessed that hair could have so much meaning? Hair can express many things . . . but most of all, hair can be BEAUTIFUL! It can make you look and feel good, just like a new coat or dress can. Think of all the things that people throughout history have done to make their hair attractive. They've powdered, curled, permed, dyed, frizzed, streaked, straightened, and even baked it! Yes, baked it! In making their wigs, the ancient Egyptians wound hair on wooden sticks, covered it with mud, and heated it over a fire.

People go to a lot of trouble to have beautiful hair! They decorate it with all kinds of things: pearls,

Mangbetu woman, Zaire
Traditionally, Mangbetu women arranged thin braids over a light, cylinder-shaped metal frame. They then decorated it with long needles made of bone. Such hairstyles took hours to achieve, and were left untouched for weeks.

Hair salon, China
Hairdressing is an ancient art, respected all over the world. In ancient Rome, people could get their hair cut at the marketplace or the public baths. In ancient Egypt, wealthy people had hairdressers come right to their house every morning. In Nigeria today, hairdressers cut hair outside, under a shady tree. In Europe and the United States, people go to beauty salons to have their hair done. Some people go once a week!

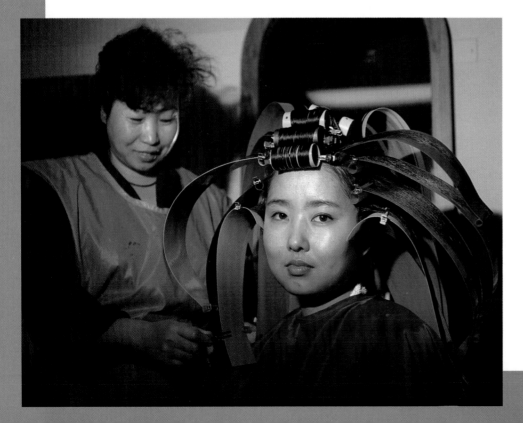

ribbons, shells, flowers, feathers, mud, eggshells, grass . . . you name it! The Masai and Samburu of Kenya and Tanzania build up their hair with red clay and thread. The Igbo of Nigeria shave their heads, allow the hair to grow a half an inch, and then cut it into geometric patterns. In Angola, women put butter in their hair to keep it glossy, and then dye it with a red powder made from tree bark. And in Papua New Guinea, the Mount Hagen people spend a long time making a special wig called a *koem* out of fur, leaves, and . . . dead beetles!

What about you? What do *you* do to your hair to make it look nice?

Colorado Indian boy, Ecuador
Men and boys of the Colorado people dye their hair with a red paste made from the achiote nut.

American boy, Tucson, Arizona

Hair salon, New York City
Some people *really* like to get creative with their hair!

international Hair

In the twentieth century, people around the world began to communicate with each other more than ever before. Because of such inventions as the radio, television, telephone, and airplane, we are now much closer to our neighbors. We can exchange ideas, share customs, and, SWAP HAIRSTYLES! Yes, hair is becoming international! A boy in Brazil may wear his hair just like a boy in Singapore. A girl in Prague may wear her hair just like a British rock star.

Now *that's* magic!

Braids around the world
Some hairstyles, such as braids, seem to crop up all over the world! One can find them everywhere from Guatemala (above), to the United States, Bangladesh, and Germany.

Japanese teenagers with British punk hairstyles

United States

Bangladesh

Germany

Cornrows Cornrowed hair, a style that originated in Africa, is now worn by people all over the world.

United States

Bahamas

Glossary

allegiance loyalty to a person, group, or cause (p.23)

ancestors relatives who lived in the past (p.5)

civilization a complex society with a stable food supply, division of labor, some form of government, and a highly developed culture (p.16)

conventional descriptive of a style or way that has been established by custom (p.23)

conservative favoring a policy of keeping things as they are; opposed to change (p.24)

culture the beliefs and customs of a group of people that are passed from one generation to another (p.5)

elaborate having much detail (p.9)

fashion the style that is popular at a particular time (p.10)

fidelity faithfulness (p.15)

gender whether a person is male or female (p.22)

generation a group of people who were born about the same time (p.24)

heritage something that is passed on from one's ancestors (p.26)

humility the quality of not being proud (p.20)

international relating to or affecting two or more nations (p.30)

misfortune bad luck (p.27)

modesty the quality of being pure and decent in thought, conduct, and dress (p.20)

mourner one who feels sorrow about a person's death (p.26)

nomadic referring to people who move from place to place (p.10)

obedient willing to obey (p.19)

prosperous successful (p.16)

radical extreme; departing from the usual or traditional (p.25)

rebellious refusing to go along with those in control (p.23)

sanitary relating to health or hygiene (p.18)

self-sufficient able to take care of oneself (p.16)

social status the position or rank of a person within his or her society (p.16)

spiritual religious (p.21)

symbolize to stand for or represent something (p.13)

traditional handed down from generation to generation (p.8)

unconventional different from the usual or ordinary (p.23)

values the ideas and ways of behaving that are viewed as important by a group of people (p.25)

vanity the quality of caring a lot about one's physical appearance (p.20)

Index

About the Author

Karin Luisa Badt has a Ph.D. in comparative literature from the University of Chicago and a B.A. in literature and society from Brown University. She likes to travel and live in foreign countries. Ms. Badt has taught at the University of Rome and the University of Chicago.